Part of a long white sampler dated 'MP 1667' in the Royal Scottish Museum. The top band shows drawn thread work. The second band consists of surface embroidery in bullion stitch. The two lower bands are cutwork, where threads have been withdrawn to make a grid of squares, to form a base for needlemade lace stitches.

AYRSHIRE
AND OTHER WHITEWORK

CONTENTS

*Published by Shire Publications Ltd, Midland House, West Way, Botley, Oxford OX2 0PH, UK. Website: www.shirebooks.co.uk
Copyright © 1982 by Margaret Swain. First published 1982; reprinted 1985, 1990 and 2001. Transferred to digital print on demand 2011. Shire Library 88. ISBN 978 0 85263 589 6.*

Printed in Great Britain by PrintOnDemand-Worldwide.com, Peterborough, UK.

Cover: *The crown of a baby cap in Ayrshire needlework. The cap is illustrated on page 21 (top right).*

A white linen bed sheet, embroidered with satin stitch and drawn thread work. It is inscribed in hair 'The Sheet off my dear, dear Lord's Bed in the wretched Tower of London February 1716. Ann C. of Derwent-waters'. The Earl of Derwentwater was executed on Tower Hill on 24th February 1716 for his part in the Jacobite rising.

A detail on a fine muslin apron, said to have been worn at the christening in exile of Prince Charles Edward Stuart in 1721. Inscribed 'God bless and restore the King to his oune', the two angels hold a royal crown over the cipher I8 for James VIII, the prince's father (the Old Pretender).

INTRODUCTION

White on white embroidery is not merely an alternative to lace: it preceded lace. The decoration of white fabric with a thread of its own colour has been practised in every age in most civilisations. This book gives a short account of the whitework most likely to be encountered in museums and salerooms. In so brief a space, it has not been possible to include rare ancient types, or such national techniques as Hardanger, Hedebo and Philippine work.

LINEN

White linen is one of the most ancient of fabrics, mentioned in the Bible. The linen fibre, flax, spins to a smooth lustrous thread; it bleaches readily in the sun and can be woven into a cool supple cloth on the most primitive of looms. It could be enriched by embroidery, using threads from the fabric. The edge could be fringed and knotted into intricate patterns, brought to Europe from Arabic countries and developed into what is now known as *macramé*. Threads could be easily withdrawn, the exposed warp or weft held in groups by stitches to form regular patterns in *drawn thread work*, or *punto tirato*. Warp and weft threads could be withdrawn to form a grid, the square holes overcast and filled with stitchery to become *cutwork (reticello)*, the earliest form of needlemade lace. This survives as patterns on many white samplers of the seventeenth century. A final development was made when the woven ground was discarded altogether, with the thread foundation stitched to parchment, to become the forerunner of all *needlepoint lace (punto in aria)*. Another form of cutwork, found on Italian embroideries of the sixteenth and seventeenth centuries, consists of overcast punched or cut holes in firmly woven linen. This is not found on British samplers of the period but became immensely popular in the nineteenth century under the name of *broderie anglaise*.

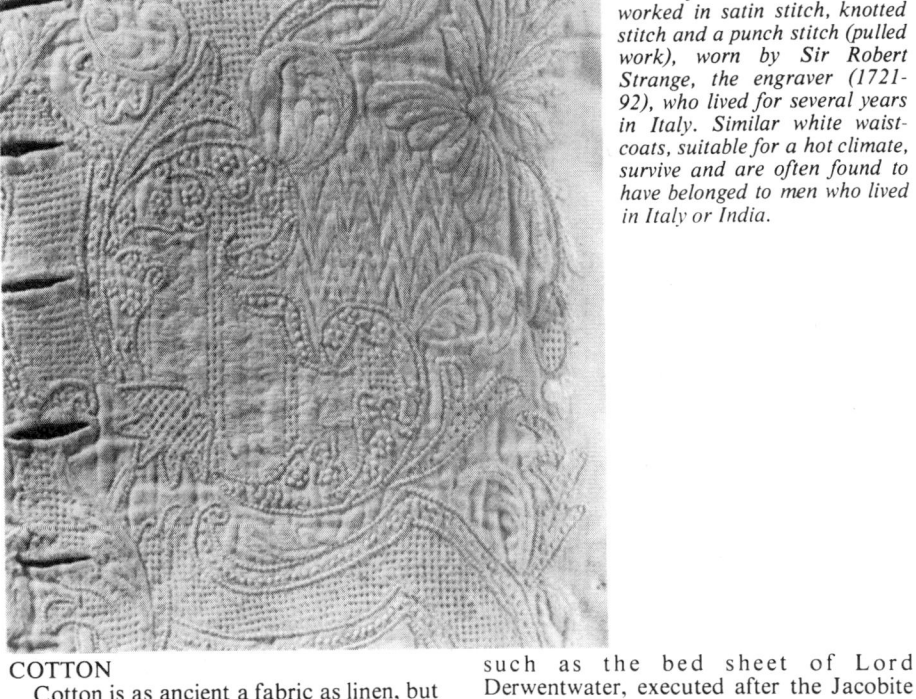

Detail of a linen twill waistcoat, worked in satin stitch, knotted stitch and a punch stitch (pulled work), worn by Sir Robert Strange, the engraver (1721-92), who lived for several years in Italy. Similar white waistcoats, suitable for a hot climate, survive and are often found to have belonged to men who lived in Italy or India.

COTTON

Cotton is as ancient a fabric as linen, but it had to be imported from the east and was not generally available in Europe until the various East India companies began importing cotton cloth, chintz and muslin, at the beginning of the seventeenth century. It became highly fashionable, taxed by governments anxious to promote home industries. Only in the second half of the eighteenth century, after machinery was invented to spin a satisfactory cotton yarn in water-powered mills, did cotton muslin become cheaper and generally available. Cotton threads do not withdraw as easily as those of linen.

WHITEWORK OF THE EIGHTEENTH CENTURY

Little whitework has survived that can be dated before 1700 in Britain, though innumerable white samplers dated before that time testify to the skill and industry expended on decorating personal, ecclesiastical and household linen. Most of it has been washed to shreds, or thriftily cut up to make useful articles, especially baby clothes. Piety has preserved other pieces, such as the bed sheet of Lord Derwentwater, executed after the Jacobite rising of 1715. It may be that the embroidery, as well as its pathetic inscription worked in hair, was done later, when his countess was staying in a Brussels convent, before her early death. Embroidered bed sheets are scarcely mentioned in contemporary inventories. Another Jacobite relic, a muslin apron worn at the christening in exile of Prince Charles Edward in 1721, and now in the Burrell collection, Glasgow, is inscribed in fine thread *God bless and restore the King to his oune* with the royal arms of Scotland. The waistcoat of Sir Robert Strange (1721-92), another notable Jacobite, can scarcely have been worn in battle, though it bears a mysterious bloodstain. It was more probably worn by him in the heat of an Italian summer, for he became a respected artist and engraver, a member of the Academy of Rome, and returned to be knighted in 1787 by George III. These isolated fragments remind us of the wealth of white embroidery, for the home, the church and dress, that must have been lost to us over the centuries.

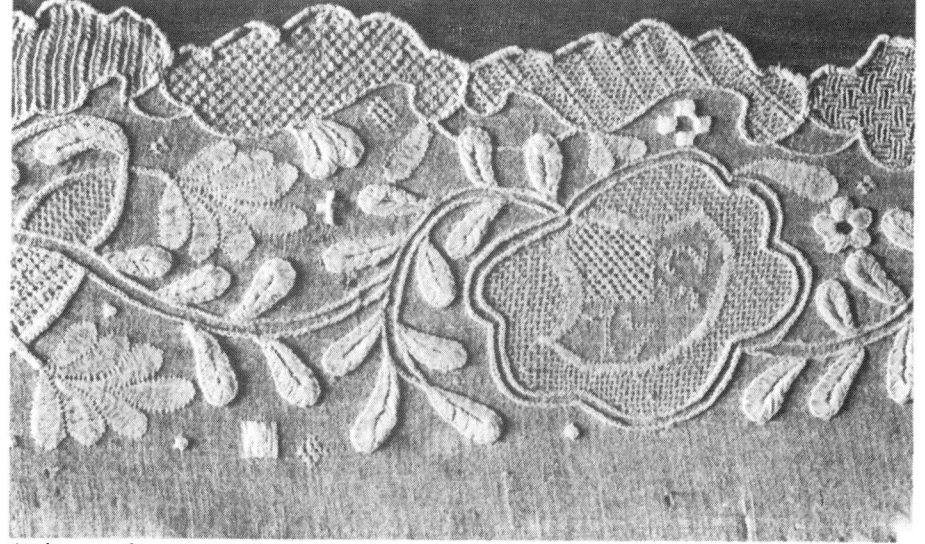

At the age of twenty-five, Miss Rachel Leonard, of Norton, Massachusetts, made this kerchief for herself in Dresden work, signing it with her initials RL in one corner, and the year 1752 (in the flower) in the other. This is a very accomplished piece by a skilled needlewoman for her own adornment.

DRESDEN WORK

With the beginning of the eighteenth century, the fine linen thread spun in the Netherlands and northern France encouraged lacemakers to devise ever more airy and diaphanous lace, with rococo designs of scrolling leaves and naturalistic flowers. Such fine lace, entailing much labour, was of necessity expensive, a visible sign of opulence. To curb extravagance, governments laid heavy duties on white lace, with the result that it became a lucrative contraband for smugglers. Not everyone could afford this enchanting but highly expensive fashion accessory. Old-fashioned cutwork was too heavy to be used in this way, but a skilled needlewoman could make a tolerable imitation by working a similar design on a piece of fine cambric or imported Indian muslin, using a variety of stitches to imitate the lace fillings. Worked under slight tension in various patterns, the fine yarn pulled the warp or weft together, leaving spaces which gave an airy lightness to the work.

This *pulled work,* as it is now called, or *drawn fabric* stitchery (not a good term, as

no threads are withdrawn: they are merely pulled together) is still popular on evenweave linen. It was this technique that was the basis of *Dresden work,* as it was called in Britain and colonial America in the eighteenth century. A great deal was made professionally in Saxony, of which Dresden was the capital. Although made in France as well, the French name was *dentelle de Saxe,* or *point de Saxe.* It may have originated in Germany for it uses many of the stitches, counted by the thread, that appear on German convent embroideries on linen, known as *opus Teutonicum,* that now survive as medieval altar cloths. It was believed that the best work came from Germany, and travellers brought home ruffles from Dresden, while in 1767 Lady Mary Coke bought muslin and sent it to Hanover to be worked.

It was made in Scandinavia as well, where much survives. Some British museums used mistakenly to label Danish work of this type *Tonder lace,* to the bewilderment of visiting Danes, who know that Tonder lace is a bobbin lace,

something like Mechlin or Buckinghamshire. White muslin samplers showing the different fillings worked in neat rectangles are found in many Scandinavian museums. The earliest, dated 1678, is in Stockholm, and there are many others dated 1800 to 1820 in Stockholm and Copenhagen.

Between 1750 and 1800 Dresden work was taught in schools for young ladies in Britain and colonial America, as their advertisements make clear. It was the type of work a neat-fingered domestic needlewoman could and did make for herself. Some even initialled and dated the piece, like the apron signed *1717 Mary Tyrell in the 14th year of her age,* and the fichu made by Rachel Leonard in Massachusetts in 1752. Dresden work decorated ruffles for sleeves and shirts, aprons, fichus, cap crowns and lappets *(barbes).* In Cleveland, Ohio, there is even an altar cloth in this technique.

The most expensive designs were professionally drawn, but at home anyone who could draw was commandeered to sketch out designs. In the schoolroom at Balcarres, Fife, in the 1760s, even the boys produced tolerable efforts for their elder sisters to work, under the direction of their governess, who came from a family of artists. The designs were drawn in ink on to stiff paper, to which the muslin was tacked for working. An unfinished piece in Brussels shows the method clearly.

The ground material was either sheer linen cambric, or, much more common, fine cotton muslin. This must have been Indian muslin if worked before about 1780, after which British muslin was manufactured in quantity. In the seventeenth and eighteenth centuries much of the muslin imported into Britain from India was re-exported to the continent and the colonies. But France, the Netherlands, Sweden and Denmark, as well as Portugal, all had East India companies to compete with these imports, so that Indian muslin was freely available in Europe.

There was also *double Dresden work,* where the leaves and scrolls appear to be applied, or one layer is cut away; the *pulled* fillings are then worked on a single layer of material. Lappets and other pieces survive in this technique: it was obviously professional, not domestic.

Part of a design for a cap lappet (streamer or barbe) drawn on paper, with matching crown, by the governess of the children of Lord Balcarres about 1760, and suitable for Dresden work, with some of the fillings indicated. Overleaf she has written: 'this is the lappet and cap which I think vastly pretty.' Stitch marks show where the muslin has been tacked to it.

The back of a baby's cap entirely covered in Dresden work in a variety of fillings. The outlines are in corded quilting. About 1750.

7

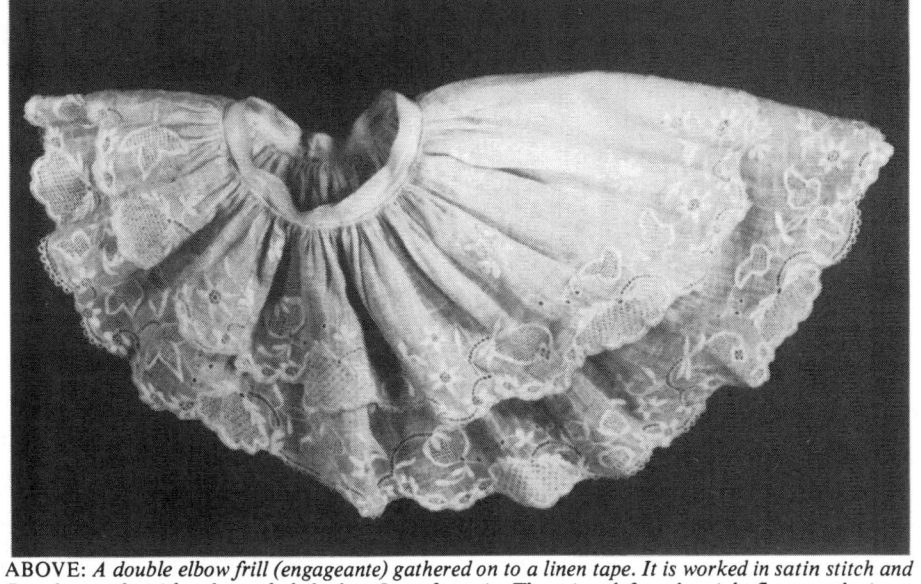

ABOVE: *A double elbow frill (engageante) gathered on to a linen tape. It is worked in satin stitch and Dresden work, with a buttonholed edge. One of a pair. There is a left and a right flounce: the inner borders are not so elaborately worked where they would rub against the body.*

BELOW: *The corner of a muslin fichu, in a delicate design of satin stitch with Dresden work fillings. The edge is finished with a strip of unheaded bobbin lace.*

When the Ladies Waldegrave were painted by Sir Joshua Reynolds in 1780, the sisters chose to be depicted around a table, with Lady Horatia holding a round tambour frame. The white muslin is held in place by a blue strap.

TAMBOUR EMBROIDERY

Chain stitch can be worked with a needle and thread, but a much more rapid method was introduced into Europe from the Orient about 1760, according to the professional French embroiderer, St Aubin, writing ten years later. This required the material to be stretched tightly over a circular frame, like the skin of a drum (French: *tambour*). The thread is held *underneath* the fabric by the left hand, while the right holds a hook, like a crochet hook, but with a sharper point. This pulls the thread up to the surface in even looped stiches, following a continuous line. Apart from its regularity, the resulting line cannot easily be distinguished from needlemade chain stitch. Diderot's *Dictionnaire des Sciences* (1763) illustrates a tambour frame

on a stand, with a leather strap holding the material firm instead of the closely fitting wooden hoop used nowadays.

Tambour work became immensely popular: 'with a little practice, the stitches are made with marvellous rapidity', and it became an elegant and easy accomplishment for fashionable ladies. Madame de Pompadour had a resplendent portrait of herself painted, wielding the tambour hook (but on a rectangular, not a circular frame). In 1781 Sir Joshua Reynolds painted the Ladies Waldegrave doing tambour work, with Lady Horatia holding a frame with a leather strap keeping the muslin taut. In *The School for Scandal* (1777) Sir Peter Teazle reminds his fashionable wife: 'I first

ABOVE: *Part of a trade sampler of tamboured muslin from Old Cumnock, Ayrshire, about 1810, showing part of a design for the hem of a lady's dress. The sampler, which is 28½ by 82 inches (724 by 2083 mm), consists of about thirty different designs, separated by wavy lines once worked in Turkey red thread, each design numbered, for borders, handkerchief corners and all-over trellis patterns worked with a tambour hook.*

BELOW: *A close-up of the border shown above. Tambour stitch is worked in a continuous line, the thread carried beneath the stretched material. The circles representing grapes are worked in solid tambour stitch. The large space has a Dresden work filling, done with needle and thread.*

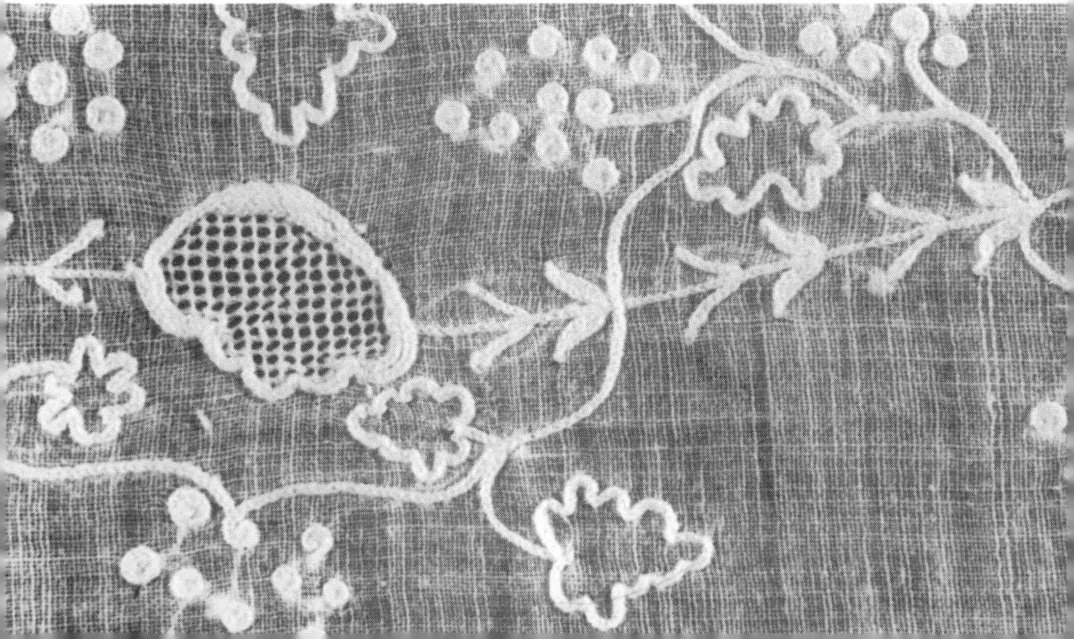

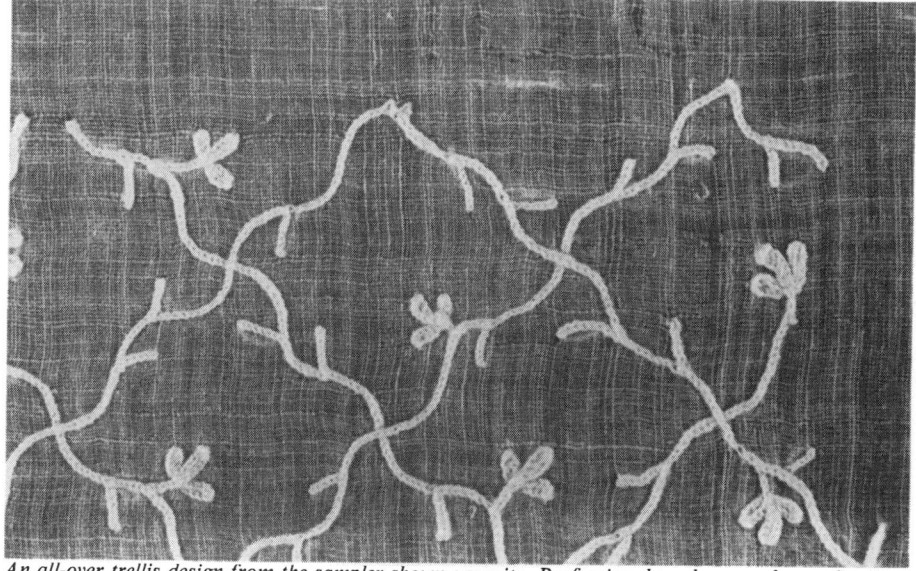

An all-over trellis design from the sampler shown opposite. Professional tambour work was done in a workroom on large frames, on which a whole width of muslin could be stretched, with girls working either side.

saw you at your tambour in a pretty figured linen gown.' Tambour work was by no means always white on white. Coloured silks were used on aprons and gentlemen's waistcoats. An Edinburgh bookseller published in 1778 *A Collection of New Patterns for the Tambour* with twelve delicately tinted designs of swags and ovals for the domestic needlewoman to follow.

PROFESSIONAL TAMBOUR EMBROIDERY

In France, as in India and China, the tambour hook was seen as a rapid way of embroidering material for sale. A great many gentlemen's coloured silk waistcoats survive, the front, pockets, buttons and buttonholes all marked out and worked in fine tambour stitch, which were never cut out and made up. These were not, of course, worked on a small round frame. Instead, the silk, ready marked, was set up in a large rectangular frame taking the whole width of material, with needlewomen seated at either side, working the nearest part.

In 1782 a professional workshop on this model was set up in Edinburgh by an Italian embroiderer, Luigi Ruffini, with twenty little girls and three boys as apprentices. He intended to undertake all types of embroidery, but the fine white cotton muslin then being manufactured in the west of Scotland (cheaper than imported Indian muslin) was eagerly bought for the flowing classical gowns fashionable at the time. Ruffini found it more profitable to concentrate on decorating this muslin with a tambour hook in flowing lines and sprigs. His male apprentices were trained to draw out suitable designs at the Drawing Academy set up by the Board of Trustees for Fisheries and Manufactures, an academy aimed at improving the standard of industrial design in Scotland. Ruffini opened another tambour workshop in Dalkeith in 1790. This was followed by others in the west of Scotland, often established by cotton manufacturers themselves, such as James Finlay, to embellish the muslin they produced for the ever increasing market. A frame of the type used in these workshops is preserved in the David Livingstone Museum, Blantyre, Lanarkshire. It is of heavy wood, table

Indian tamboured muslin, about 1900. The elephant and petals are worked in solid tambour stitch. The fine muslin was stiffened with gum arabic to hold it firm while working.

height, with rollers at either end, 44 inches wide (1117 mm), held by ratchets. It was capable of holding a full web of muslin, with room for four girls, two working at either side, to cover the stamped designs with lines of tambour stitches. The design on the muslin was previously printed with a blue or pink water-soluble dye by means of wooden blocks.

Muslin was tamboured at other centres' in Britain — Manchester, Nottingham and Middlesex — though no account of this trade has yet been written. Machine-made bobbin net, which became available after 1809, made an admirably delicate ground for designs in tambour embroidery and was worked for sale in Ireland (Limerick), Coggeshall in Essex and at Brussels. Communities of the Protestant Moravian church, established by Count Zinzendorf (1700-60), also made fichus, caps and mittens in tambour stitch on net for their own use in the early nineteenth century: some is said to have been made for sale. Like needle-run net, tamboured net is properly classed as a lace.

Mrs Jamieson, wife of an Ayr cotton agent (one who gave out the yarn to handloom weavers and collected the finished webs). Mrs Jamieson taught women working in their own homes to embroider the fine cotton muslin which she distributed to them, ready stamped. Mrs Jamieson's collar and cap are of sewed muslin (Ayrshire needlework). This was called sewed muslin to distinguish it from tamboured muslin.

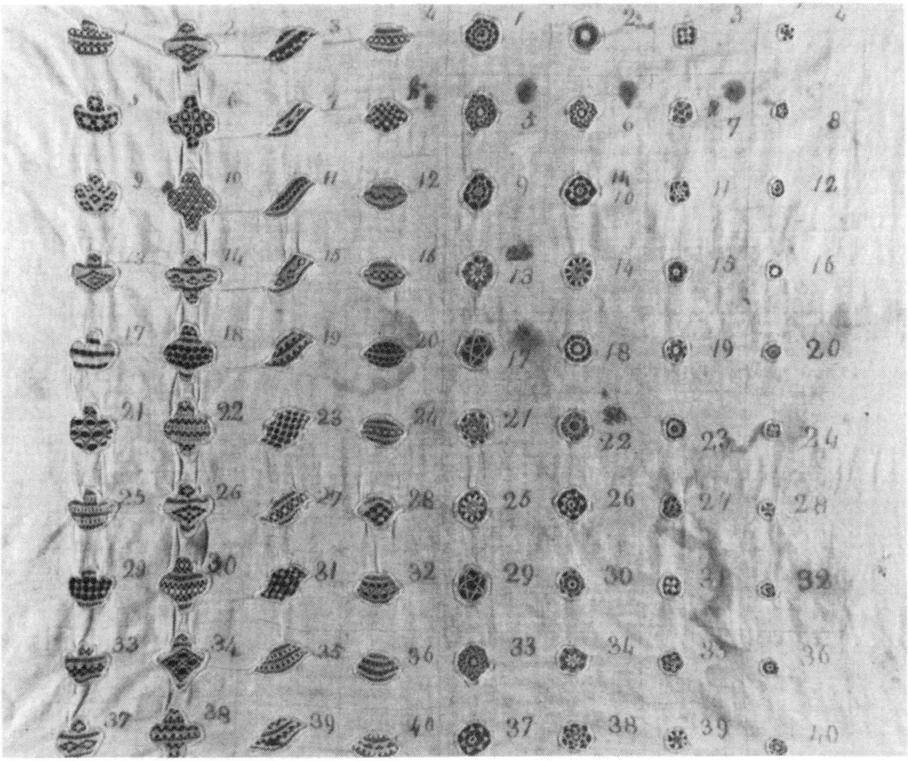

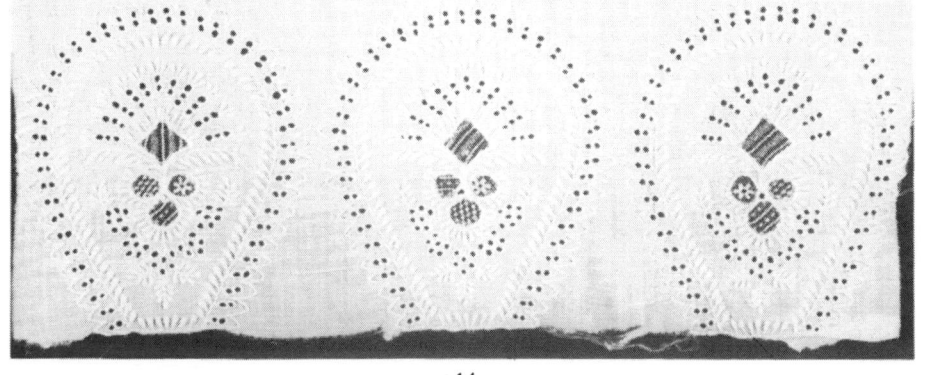

ABOVE: *A worker's sampler, from Ayrshire, of lace stitches suitable for variously shaped spaces. The ordinary worker could earn a shilling a day if she worked steadily; those who specialised in lace stitches earned slightly more, hence the cost of a dress or cap depended on the amount of lace insets.*

BELOW: *The crowns of babies' caps were not always circular, as this uncut piece, worked on muslin, not the customary cambric, shows. They came from the stock of Alexander Wylie, sewed muslin manufacturer, Glasgow (flourished 1790-1839). Instead of the usual lace-stitch insets, darned net has been substituted, probably because no lace specialist was available in the area in which they were worked.*

Wooden blocks with copper strips inserted, used for stamping embroidery designs on to muslin. The design of the larger block is a continuous line and it could be used for tamboured muslin. The spaces on the smaller block could be filled with lace stitches for sewed muslin (Ayrshire needlework). Scottish, 1840-50.

AYRSHIRE NEEDLEWORK

During the Napoleonic wars (1796-1815) there were many fluctuations in the cotton trade in Britain, and the tamboured muslin industry suffered accordingly. At the end of the war, the simple muslin gown went out of fashion and a new mode, with wide shoulders and small waist, in brighter colours, developed. White muslin was now used for wide collars called *pelerines* and for ladies' indoor caps embellished with bunches of frilling. This called for a different type of embroidery, delicate, but with more body than the rather limp sheer effect of Dresden work or tamboured muslin. In this, Britain followed Paris, for it was a European fashion, and each country produced its own version.

The Scottish muslin manufacturers produced a firmer muslin, and a new type of embroidery evolved. This was devised by the wife of an Ayr cotton agent, Mrs Jamieson, who had been lent a French baby robe brought back by the widowed Lady Mary Montgomerie, mother of the thirteenth Earl of Eglinton. Mrs Jamieson taught outworkers, mostly farmers' wives and daughters, the firm satin stitch, the overcast fillings and, above all, the fine lace stitches made with needle and thread in the cut-out spaces that are so characteristic of this beautiful craft. Mrs Jamieson, helped by her two daughters, was an excellent organiser. No poor work was tolerated, and it had to be finished in time. Those who specialised in the fine lace-stitch fillings, worked after the other embroidery was completed, were paid at a higher rate. The designs were drawn out by professional male draughtsmen (pattern drawers) in Glasgow, and the completed embroidery was sent back there to be bleached, made up, boxed and marketed.

This embroidery, called *sewed muslin,* to distinguish it from plain muslin and tamboured muslin, became popularly known as *Ayrshire embroidery* after the county of its origin. It was widely marketed and exported to other countries, notably to north America. To meet the demand, the Glasgow cotton manufacturers sent the stamped designs to workers in surrounding counties in Scotland, and also to northern Ireland, where many women became adept in the technique. Miles of flouncing, stamped in blue water-soluble dye by means of wooden blocks or rollers, were produced for frills for women's caps and men's shirts, for collars and cuffs, handkerchiefs and other fashion accessories. Little of this survives, but the baby robes, made as day robes for the offspring of prosperous families, have in

ABOVE: *An Ayrshire baby robe now in Canada. The triangular point of the bodice was traditionally worn outside, as here, by a baby boy, but tucked inside the waist band for a girl. About 1869.*
OPPOSITE: *The skirt of the robe shown above. This handsome solid design of fern leaves is typical of the taste of the late 1860s and was drawn by a professional designer, working in Glasgow. This was not intended merely as a christening robe but was a day dress, as opposed to the plain night dress.*

many cases been preserved out of sentiment, often with the cap with its decorated crown. They are still treasured as family christening robes, though the laundering of these garments is a daunting task.

The style of the robe echoes the fashionable lady's dress of the late 1830s, with its inverted triangle for the bodice, its puffed off-the-shoulder sleeves and long triangular panel in the front of the skirt, flanked by *robings,* a flat frill on either side. As well as the completed baby dresses, it was possible to buy the embroidered bodice pieces and cap crowns, so that the domestic needlewoman could make up the layette herself.

The craft of Ayrshire embroidery was severely damaged by the American Civil War (1861-5). The blockade imposed by the northern states effectively cut off the supply of raw cotton from the southern states to Britain. The Lancashire cotton industry finally recovered, but the Scottish muslin trade never completely revived. More damaging still, the cheaper Swiss machine embroidery, which at first imitated the eyelet holes and lace-stitch 'wheels' of white Ayrshire needlework, was able to undercut the Scottish handwork, especially in the United States.

During this period continental firms, particularly the French, were able to capture the market. Even the Franco-Prussian War was no deterrent. In January 1871, the *Milliner, Dressmaker and Warehousemen's Gazette* could report from London: 'We are happy to find the trade in white embroidery, both hand and machine, is uninterrupted (by the siege of Paris) and that MM Achille Blaize et Cie can fill orders to any extent in these goods. Among the lovely specimens of broderie shown, we note an immense variety of designs . . . Perfection of embroidery is shown on the lovely robes prepared for infants, which are repeats of the designs

which gained gold medals at the French and American exhibitions. These robes are wonderfully beautiful, worked entirely by hand, and selling at marvellously low prices. . .'

The sewed muslin industry was unable to recover from this double competition, Swiss and French. Young women no longer learned to flower muslin. Older workers eked out a living by working the coarser, firmer eyelet holes of the so called *broderie anglaise* and when they died no one took their place in what had become a depressed, poorly paid occupation.

LEFT: *Detail of a baby robe, bought in Glasgow, with fillings of darned net instead of needle lace stitches.*

BELOW: *Fashions for September 1839. The baby robes were miniature versions of this fashion and stayed the same till the end of the century, with off the shoulder neckline and flat frills on either side of the triangular skirt panel.*

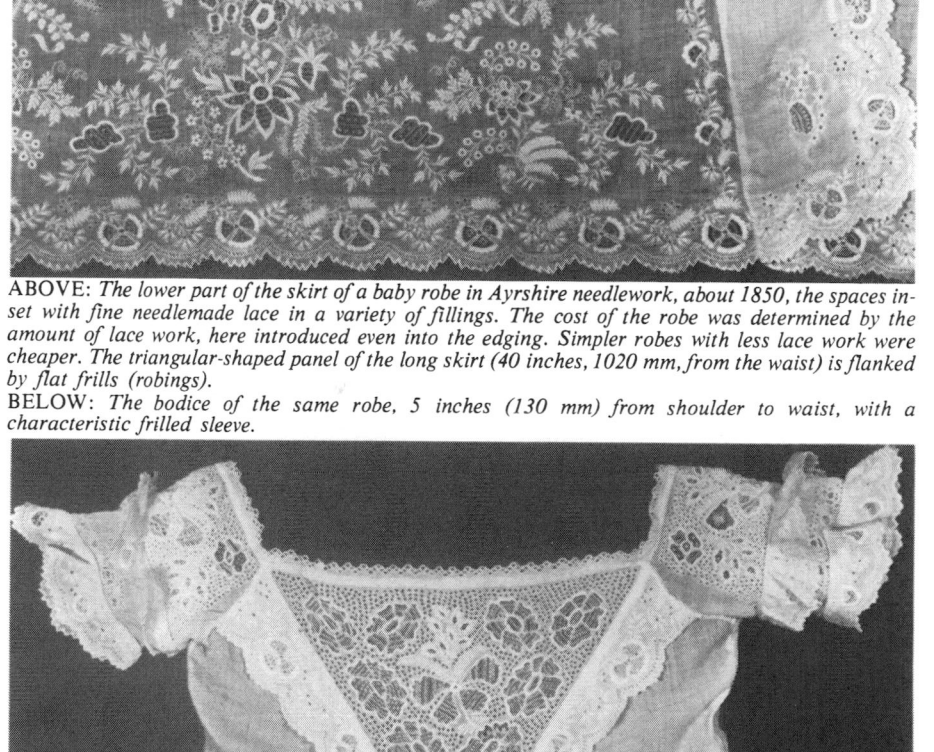

ABOVE: *The lower part of the skirt of a baby robe in Ayrshire needlework, about 1850, the spaces inset with fine needlemade lace in a variety of fillings. The cost of the robe was determined by the amount of lace work, here introduced even into the edging. Simpler robes with less lace work were cheaper. The triangular-shaped panel of the long skirt (40 inches, 1020 mm, from the waist) is flanked by flat frills (robings).*
BELOW: *The bodice of the same robe, 5 inches (130 mm) from shoulder to waist, with a characteristic frilled sleeve.*

LEFT: *An uncut worked bodice for a baby robe. The muslin, marked out and stamped with the design, was given to the needlewomen (the 'flowerers') to be embroidered. When completed, it was returned to be made up, laundered and boxed.*

BELOW: *A detail showing the sleeve cap and narrow edging of the baby robe above. It was possible to buy pieces like this ready embroidered, to be made up at home.*

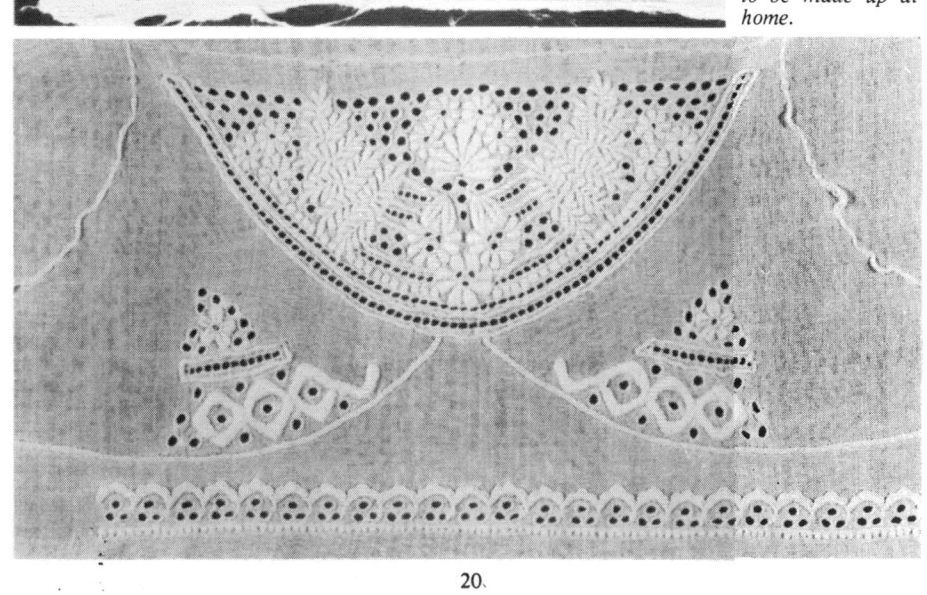

ABOVE LEFT: *The crown of a woman's cap, French, nineteenth century. It is often difficult to distinguish between pieces of French origin and Ayrshire needlework. Ayrshire needlework is characterised by the wide variety of fillings in the best pieces (see the worker's sampler on page 14). The French embroidery is usually worked on a cambric foundation (but see the baby cap, right).*

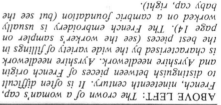

ABOVE RIGHT: *A baby cap in Ayrshire needlework. The caps are almost always worked on fine cambric, thought to be cooler than cotton for the infant's head. The front was drawn up by fine cords and decorated with lace frills and loops of narrow picot ribbon. The crown of the cap is illustrated on the front cover. Crowns could be bought separately to be made up at home: often the whole cap is the gift of friendship or the preparation of affection, says the writer of 'Baby Linen', published in 1843. This was a day cap, worn by an infant in arms. Night caps, worn in the cot, were of plain cambric.*

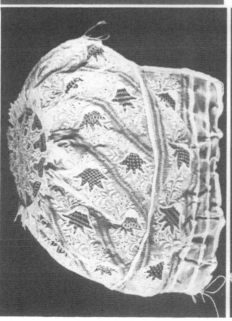

RIGHT: *A baby's cap in Ayrshire needlework worn by a baby born in Glasgow in 1847. It is trimmed with two rows of frills of bobbin lace and picot ribbon. Instead of the usual pink or blue, this baby wore black, as her mother died at her birth.*

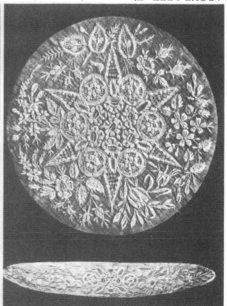

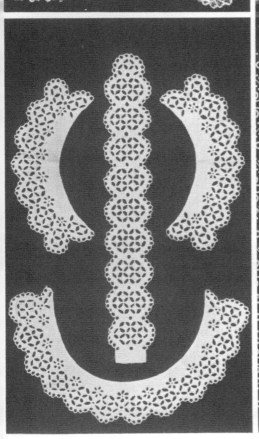

ABOVE LEFT: A design for an embroidered muslin petticoat for Queen Victoria. In 1861, following the bankruptcy of several Glasgow firms, Queen Victoria sought to alleviate hardship and stimulate demand by ordering dresses, trimmings, handkerchiefs and caps for herself and her daughters, made from the latest designs sent from Paris.

ABOVE RIGHT: A collar and cuffs, with neck tab, worked on calico in broderie anglaise, from Irvine, Ayrshire.

RIGHT: Not all Ayrshire embroidery was made for costume, as this charming lace-edged pin-cushion, made for the dressing table, shows. It was part of the stock of Mrs and Miss Bowie, muslin printers and embroiderers, Princes Street, Edinburgh, a business that flourished from 1839 to 1939. This was made about 1860.

Uncut petticoat flouncing in broderie anglaise. The design was printed on a full width of calico for working and finally cut around the scallops with fine scissors. This piece was worked by a young woman in Ayrshire, who earned sufficient by her sewing to buy her brother out of the army and so secure his earlier discharge. 1870.

BRODERIE ANGLAISE

'The broderie anglaise patterns are outlines of variously sized holes, arranged to make floral or geometrical devices. Embroidery cotton is run around these outlines, they are then pierced with a stiletto or cut with scissors, their edges turned under and sewn over with embroidery cotton' (Caulfeild and Saward 1882). This required a firm foundation — calico or Irish linen — and was used for underwear, dress and household linen from 1850 onwards. The *Milliner, Dressmaker and Warehousemen's Gazette* of August 1871 reported: 'It is strange that after a lapse of nearly ten years, a perfect *furore* for English embroidery should obtain. The title of broderie anglaise is given to all kinds of openwork embroidery (in distinction from satin stitch embroidery) whether of Swiss, Scotch, Irish or really English production.'

A close-up of the central panel of a baby robe, cut like an Ayrshire robe but made in India. An attempt has been made to fill the circular spaces with 'wheels', but the filling of the larger spaces is made with a characteristic Indian 'punch' stitch, worked diagonally, as the needlemade lace stitches were outside the experience of the Indian embroiderer.

INDIAN WHITEWORK

Many of the baby dresses decorated with Ayrshire needlework were sent out to India to British wives expecting their firstborn: indeed, whole layettes could be purchased for as little as £20 in the 1850s. As the family increased, the embroidered robe was used as a pattern for subsequent offspring, and many of these Indian-made robes survive. They are often good copies of the Scottish sewed muslin designs, but as the Indian embroiderer did not have the technique of the lace-stitch fillings, a characteristic 'punch' stitch, worked with a thicker needle, with thread at tension, was used instead. This stitch, worked diagonally, called *Jali*, serves to identify Indian-made robes, in all other respects cut and made up as an Ayrshire robe.

Chikan is a type of Indian whitework that originated in Lucknow, but during the nineteenth century it spread to Calcutta and Madras. Some of the designs are unmistakably Indian but, in order to cater for the British in India, European designs became more profitable. Worked on an open Indian muslin, stoles and shawls, as well as handkerchiefs, found a ready market and were often taken home as gifts.

MADEIRA WORK

Just as sewed muslin, or Ayrshire embroidery, owed its origin to French needlework, so the Madeira embroidery industry derived from Scotland. In 1858, after the phylloxera disease had decimated the vines of Madeira, causing great hardship due to the loss of their chief export, the daughter of an English wine importer, Miss Phelps, engaged a Scotswoman to teach the Ayrshire technique to women on the island. The hot climate caused the workers' fingers to become damp, so a characteristic blue yarn was introduced, and linen, not cotton, formed the ground. When white embroidery no longer found a sale, colour was introduced, and other styles, more typical of Portugal, of which Madeira forms a part, were adopted.

WHITE MACHINE EMBROIDERY

Attempts were made by muslin weavers in Scotland to invent ways of 'flowering' the material, to decorate it mechanically during the process of weaving, but none were commercially successful. A *Patent Tambour Machine* was invented by John Duncan, author of *Essays on the Art of Weaving* (Glasgow, 1807), with 'a row of hooks replacing the human hand'. The first effective embroidery machine was made in Mulhouse, Alsace, in 1828 by Josua Heilmann. One of these machines was sold to a firm in St Gallen, Switzerland, and it was the Swiss who perfected the manufacture of white machine embroidery, based on the designs that the Glasgow merchants had exported so successfully. The first consignment of Swiss embroidery was sent to New York in 1855, called *Hamburgs* from its port of exit. A Swiss firm even set up an office in Glasgow itself in 1856.

The early white machine embroidery was of extremely high quality and is often mistaken for Ayrshire needlework. It was generally worked with a well twisted thread, even imitating the open 'wheels' of sewed muslin. Like all machine embroidery, it can be identified by examining the back and noting where the thread passes over to the next motif. In hand embroidery, even where the needlewoman works with great regularity, a needleful of thread ends at different places. In machine embroidery, with its row of needles working in unison, the threads all pass to the next motif in exactly the same place.

A close-up of machine embroidery seen from the back. The machines consisted of a row of double-ended needles, working in unison on each repeat. The thread of each passes to the next motif at precisely the same place. A hand worker cannot sustain this regularity, as the thread ends and is finished off at different places.

ABOVE: *A flounce of white machine embroidery on cotton, probably Swiss. The design follows those made popular by the Scottish sewed muslin industry, even to the 'wheel' filling of the circular holes, punched out in advance. Instead of the fine soft yarn used in hand embroidery, a fairly thick twisted yarn is used to cover the ground quickly.*

BELOW: *A corner of a pillow sham (the daytime cover for an exposed pillow) made of smooth cotton jean and edged with a cotton fringe. It is worked with Mountmellick embroidery in a soft cotton yarn in well padded satin stitch, stem and buttonhole stitch and French knots. The blackberries were a favourite motif on Mountmellick work. About 1880.*

MOUNTMELLICK EMBROIDERY

Ayrshire needlework was essentially a fashion accessory, although an occasional piece survives that was not intended for costume, as, for instance, the two bedspreads made for the Countess of Eglinton, a patron of the craft, in 1863. Mountmellick embroidery, on the other hand, appeared chiefly on household linens: tray cloths, mats, toilet covers, bedspreads and 'pillow shams' (daytime covers to place over the exposed pillow). It owes nothing to Ayrshire needlework and was usually worked on cotton jean, or other firm material, in a thick soft yarn, mostly in raised stitches, such as well padded satin stitch and French knots.

It is said to have been started by Mrs Joanna Carter at Mountmellick, Ireland, about 1825, but the craft appears to have declined after her death. In 1880 an Industrial Society of Mountmellick was established to give employment to local women and to market their work. Most of the surviving pieces show designs typical of this later period: well drawn naturalistic raised sprays of flowers, berries and seeds. *Weldon's Practical Needlework,* an annual publication started in 1886, published Mountmellick designs for the amateur needlewoman in volume 4 (1890), volume 5 (1891), volume 8 (1894) and volume 12 (1898).

RICHELIEU EMBROIDERY

Richelieu embroidery is a Victorian name for a type of cutwork worked on firm linen, where the design is composed of scrolls and leaves, outlined with close buttonhole stitch, joined by overcast or buttonhole bars, the spaces then cut away with fine scissors. *The Dictionary of Needlework* (Caulfeild and Saward, 1882) describes

Richelieu guipure as 'work of a modern date, founded upon the ancient point coupé or cutwork'. Although generally whitework, the buttonhole outline was sometimes worked in a contrasting cotton or silk. It was fashionable for collars and cuffs, tray cloths and table linen from the 1850s to the 1930s.

A corner of a linen tray cloth in Richelieu work. The design is outlined in buttonhole stitch on linen, the ground cut away, and the points secured by buttonhole bars. About 1930.

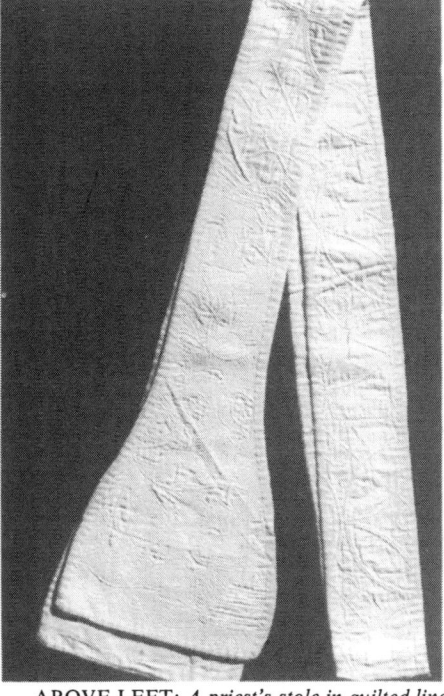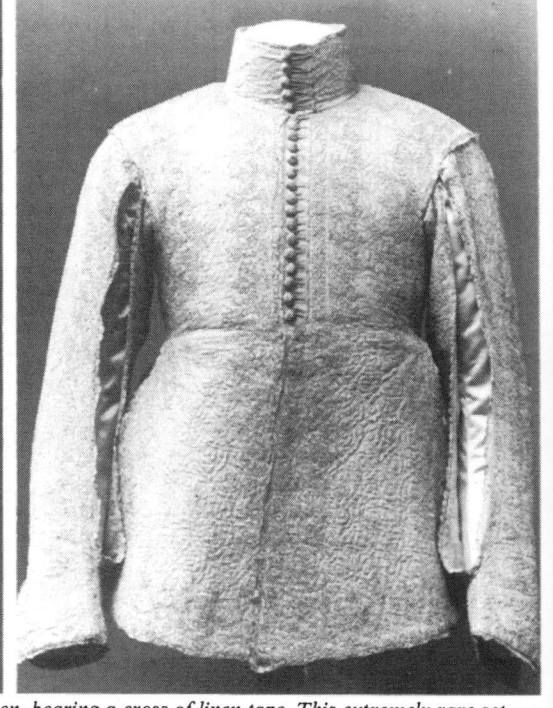

ABOVE LEFT: *A priest's stole in quilted linen, bearing a cross of linen tape. This extremely rare set of chasuble, altar frontal, stoles and chalice veil has been made from a white linen quilt. In 1688 a Protestant mob ransacked the Roman Catholic mansion of Traquair, Peeblesshire, destroying all altar furnishings from the chapel. This set, still in the house, was probably made to replace the destroyed vestments and could be folded to look like household linen, if a similar raid took place.*

ABOVE RIGHT: *A quilted linen doublet of the 1630s, richly decorated with a design of applied knotted cord (stringwork). Knotting became very fashionable by the end of the seventeenth century and was worked with a shuttle, like a tatting shuttle, but with more open ends.*

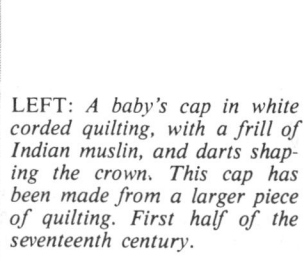

LEFT: *A baby's cap in white corded quilting, with a frill of Indian muslin, and darts shaping the crown. This cap has been made from a larger piece of quilting. First half of the seventeenth century.*

QUILTING

Quilting is essentially functional; it is the stitching together of two layers of fabric, with or without a padding between. It is an ancient craft, found in the east as well as the west. Quilted caps and short kilts survive, worn by Roman soldiers beneath armour. Quilting requires a frame to hold the layers evenly together. It is basically plain sewing — running stitch or back stitch — but the most beautiful and intricate designs have been achieved by the simplest means, using saucers or wineglasses for circles and cardboard templates for curves. Decorative patterns are made by rows of stitches, given a sculptured appearance by the padding. This may be a layer of teased sheep's wool, cotton wool, flannel or domett. Alternatively thick woollen yarn may be drawn through parallel lines (*Italian quilting*, or *trapunto*), or the parallel lines may be worked in reverse herringbone stitch, enclosing a wick or cord (*English quilting*). This last requires great precision and is mostly found on articles made in the eighteenth century: waistcoats, baby caps, toilet covers.

Because a large frame was often required, quilting was frequently produced professionally. Quilted petticoats and jackets could be purchased in the eighteenth century. During the nineteenth century, quilting became a cottage industry in Wales and Durham, revived in the 1930s. This specialisation gave rise to great skill and some handsome designs. In the United States, where the patchwork quilt evolved from an article of thrift to a popular art of great beauty, 'quilting bees', where several quilters sat round a frame to finish a quilt, were festive occasions in country social life.

Quilting is not necessarily whitework. The quilting is often worked in yellow silk, like the *muga* silk of Indian embroidery, and may indeed have been imported ready quilted from India for the domestic needlewoman to add coloured embroidery of her own choice. It appears, of course, on coloured fabrics such as patchwork quilts, but the most beautiful effect is that of white on white.

STRINGWORK

Occasionally a piece of whitework is found, often browned with age, that appears to be embroidered with the sinuous curves of a knotted stitch. Close examination shows that this is a fine knotted cord couched (held down on the surface by stitches) in a decorative pattern to linen or twill, occasionally to silk or satin with a firm backing.

In the seventeenth and eighteenth centuries the knotting of fine cords to apply as decoration to costume or bedcovers became a fashionable pursuit. Thin round thread or cord was wound on to a shuttle like a tatting shuttle, but with more open ends, the knots being made at regular intervals, the resulting knotted cord fed into a bag suspended over the left wrist. Queen Mary, the wife of William III, was satirised for her addiction to knotting. In 1766 Mrs Delany (1700 - 88) wrote to her niece: 'I have a pound of such knotting thread as I make use of; but if it is too coarse, let me

know and I will get you some finer. . .this is six shillings a pound English'. The following year she bought 'a very elegant *shuttle* for two guineas. . .' ('*Cotton* thread is not strong enough to bear the working.') A coverlet of white linen, decorated with an all-over design of knotting, worked by Mrs Delany for a godson, is in the Ulster Museum, Belfast. She made a set of bed hangings, with window curtains, decorated with knotting, and even a set of chair covers, though the knotting for these may have been done in coloured wools. A set of chair covers at Cotehele in Cornwall appears to be worked in this technique, known locally as 'Queen Anne's tatting'. The daughters of King George III were accomplished knotters, and pieces of their work still survive. Knotting appears to have gone out of fashion after 1800; elegant shuttles are still to be found. They are often mistaken for tatting shuttles.

HOLLIE POINT

Perhaps this was originally 'holy' point, from the holes comprising the design, or possibly the name refers to the religious motifs it displays: the lily for purity, for example. This is strictly a point lace, made with needle and thread, and worked in rows of looped stitches with spaces to form the design. Although used mostly for baby caps and shirts, it should not be confused with Ayrshire embroidery. The strips of lace form an insertion to join the pieces of fine linen cambric, considered the necessary first layer for the fine skin of an infant. It is believed to have been popular in Tudor times, though little if any of this period has survived. It appears on samplers in England, Scotland and Scandinavia right up to the 1820s.

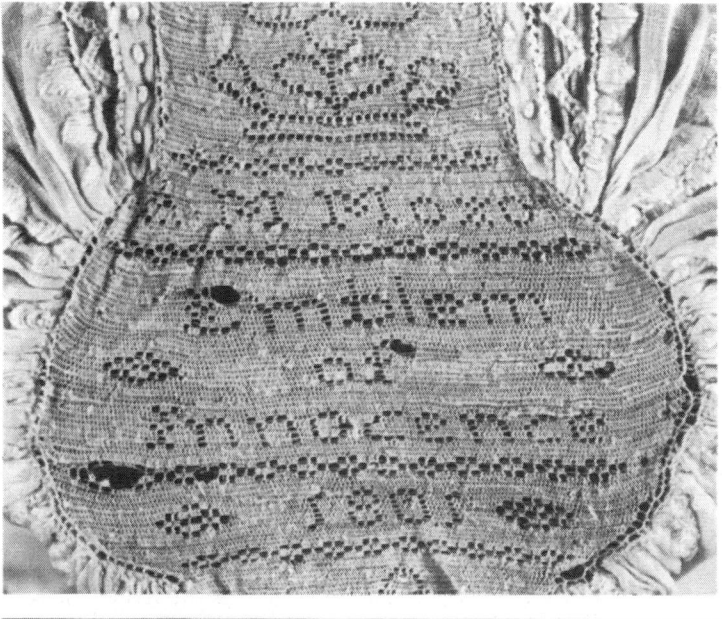

LEFT: *A strip of hollie point forming the crown of a cambric baby cap, inscribed 'A. M. Moxon Emblem of Innocence 1801'. The design is worked by leaving holes in the rows of looped stitches.*

BELOW: *Samples of handkerchief initials, with prices (2s, 2s 6d) on fine Irish linen, prepared by a Belfast firm about 1900. The embroidering of handkerchiefs and household linen to order was given out to workers who did it in their own homes.*

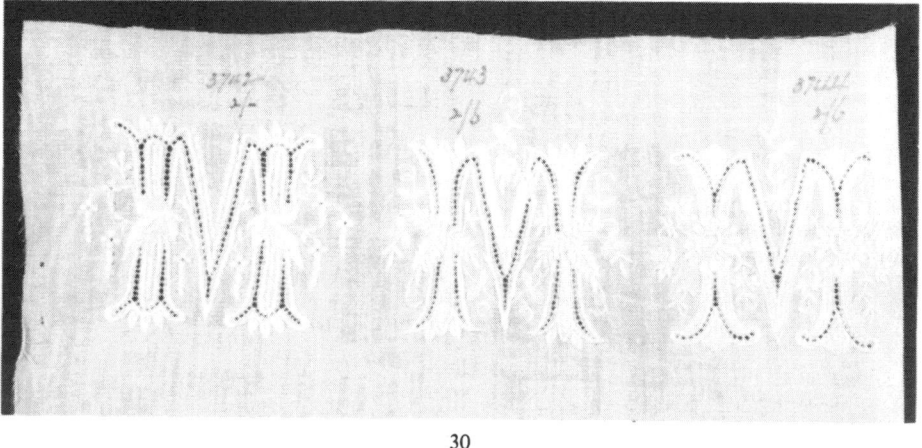

30

Perhaps the most beautiful and accomplished panel of whitework in Britain. The royal arms, with the Prince of Wales's feathers, were worked by Lady Evelyn Stuart Murray, younger daughter of the seventh Duke of Atholl, about 1912 and may be seen at Blair Castle, Perthshire, together with the trial pieces. It is worked in cotton on sheer cambric and measures 22 by 25 inches (560 by 635 mm).

CONCLUSION

Like Ayrshire needlework, much white on white embroidery was produced professionally, either in workrooms, or given to outworkers to complete to a required standard and in a stipulated time. The trade of the *lingère* in France, often in the hands of women, has always been distinct from that of the *brodeur*, the professional embroiderer. It was the *lingère* who supplied the delicately embroidered handkerchiefs, underwear, baby clothes and household linen, so sought after for their design and finish.

It should be remembered, however, that any dedicated neat-fingered needlewoman, then as now, could and did reproduce these designs and techniques, either for her own use or for sale. Religious communities, such as the Moravian sisters or nuns in convents, who made their own altar linen, frequently used this skill by selling white embroidery, often to order. The success of the enterprise depended on the designs offered. If they were old-fashioned or poorly drawn, orders were not forthcoming. If, however, they were fashionable, well executed and cheaper than the market price, there was a ready sale. This should be borne in mind when assessing a piece of whitework of unknown origin. Even if well drawn and crisply worked, it is not necessarily a professional product, as the fichu of Rachel Leonard and the panel by Lady Evelyn Stuart Murray clearly demonstrate.

FURTHER READING

Boyle, Elizabeth. *The Irish Flowerers*. Belfast, 1971.
Bryson, A.S. *Ayrshire Needlework*. Batsford, 1989.
Cave, Oenone. *Linen Cutwork*. Vista Books, 1963.
Dudding, Jean. *Coggeshall Lace*. Braintree, Essex, not dated. (For a good description of the tambour technique.)
Earnshaw, Pat. *The Identification of Lace*. Shire, reprinted 2000.
Iklé, Ernest. *La Broderie Mechanique*. Paris, 1931.
Morris, Barbara. *Victorian Embroidery*. Herbert Jenkins, 1962.
Paine, Sheila. *Chikan Embroidery*. Shire, 1989.
Swain, Margaret. *The Flowerers, the Story of Ayrshire White Needlework*. W. and R. Chambers, 1955.

PLACES TO VISIT

Museums rarely display white embroidery for its own sake; it is generally regarded as a costume accessory, used to set off a garment, and frequently omitted in the description on the label. It is, therefore, generally advisable to write in advance for permission to see whitework.

UNITED KINGDOM
Blair Castle, Blair Atholl, Pitlochry, Perthshire PH18 5TL.
 Telephone: 01796 481207. Website: www.blair-castle.co.uk
Castle Howard, Castle Howard Estate Ltd, York, North Yorkshire YO60 7DA.
 Telephone: 01653 648333. Website: www.castlehoward.co.uk
Gallery of Costume, Platt Hall, Rusholme, Manchester M14 5LL. Telephone: 0161 224 5217.
Gawthorpe Hall, Burnley Road, Padiham, near Burnley, Lancashire BB12 8UA.
 Telephone: 01282 771004. Website: www.nationaltrust.org.uk
Glasgow Art Gallery and Museum, Argyle Street, Glasgow, G3 8AG. Telephone: 0141 276 9500
Guildford Museum, Castle Arch, Quarry Street, Guildford, Surrey GU1 3SX.
 Telephone: 01483 444751.
Museum of Costume, Assembly Rooms, Bennett Street, Bath BA1 2QH.
 Telephone: 01225 477789. Website: www.museumofcostume.co.uk
National Museum of Scotland, Chambers Street, Edinburgh EH1 1JF.
 Telephone: 0300 123 6789. Website: www.nms.ac.uk
Nottingham Castle Museum, The Castle, Lenton Road, Nottingham NG1 6EL.
 Telephone: 0844 4775678. Website: www.nottinghamcity.gov.uk
Stewarty Museum, St Mary Street, Kirkcudbright DG6 4AG.
 Telephone: 01557 331643. Website: www.dumfriesmuseum.demon.co.uk
Strangers' Hall Museum, Charing Cross, Norwich, Norfolk NR2 4AL.
 Telephone: 01603 493636. Website: www.visitnorfolk.co.uk
Traquair House, Innerleithen, Peeblesshire EH44 6PW.
 Telephone: 01896 830323. Website: www.traquair.co.uk
Ulster Folk and Transport Museum, Cultra Manor, Holywood, County Down, Northern Ireland
 BT18 0EU. Telephone: 02890 428428. Website: www.nmni.com/uftm
Victoria and Albert Museum, Cromwell Road, South Kensington, London SW7 2RL.
 Telephone: 020 7942 2000. Website: www.vam.ac.uk
York Castle Museum, Eye of York, York YO1 9RY.
 Telephone: 01904 687687. Website: www.yorkcastlemuseum.org.uk

OTHER COUNTRIES
Christian Decker Design Shop, The Old Court House, Evansville, Indiana 47708, USA.
Textilmuseum mit Textilbibliothek, Vadianstrasse 2, 9000 St Gallen, Switzerland.

ACKNOWLEDGEMENTS
 My thanks are due to all the private owners and museums who have generously allowed their pieces to be used as illustrations. I am especially grateful to Naomi Tarrant, who encouraged me to write this book, and to Helen Bennett and Sandra Foubister, who gave me welcome advice and support in completing it.
 Illustrations are acknowledged as follows: Burrell Collection, Glasgow, page 3; Museum of Fine Arts, Boston, page 5; Museum of London, page 2; National Galleries of Scotland, page 9; National Museum of Antiquities of Scotland, pages 4, 8 (top), 10 (both), 20 (both), 22 (bottom right), 28 (bottom); Royal Scottish Museum, page 1; Saltire Society, page 21 (bottom); Ulster Folk and Transport Museum, page 26 (bottom); Victoria and Albert Museum, page 28 (top right).